CW01467370

THIRTIESTYLE

home decoration and furnishings from the 1930s

KATIE ARBER

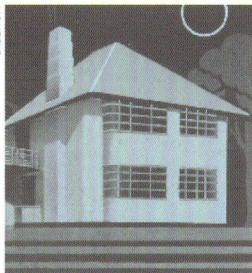

Roger Malcom Ltd,
brochure for new houses in
Edgware, 1935. Courtesy of
Roger Malcom Ltd

CONTENTS

INTRODUCTION

1930s interiors were not of one uniform style. A range of looks existed and most people, like today, selected from among what was on sale to create a unique home. There was plenty of choice in specialist shops, department stores, decorators and builders' merchants around the country.

A few people lived in architect-designed, flat-roofed houses and, in London particularly, in well-equipped flats. In the suburbs of Britain's cities and towns, speculative developers built semi-detached and detached houses in large numbers. From the outside many looked similar to houses built in the past and new architectural styles ranging from the neo-Tudor to the neo-Georgian were often seen in the same street. 'Moderne' suburban houses mixed up-to-date features like metal-framed windows with elements from the past.

Catalogue for Whiteley's, 1935
This living room was displayed at the 1935 Ideal Home Exhibition by Whiteley's, a leading London department store, and shows some key 1930s design features.
©Whiteley's

*Catalogue for Baxendale's, 1936
Baxendale's, a large furnishing store
in Manchester, offered a wide choice
of furniture and fittings of different styles.
Courtesy of Baxendale & Co. Ltd*

But all new 1930s homes offered a different and better way of living for middle-class Britons. Whatever its appearance, virtually every one came with the most modern conveniences. Electric lighting, plumbed-in bathrooms and well-equipped kitchens were included. Equally their owners aspired to decorate their new homes to reflect their modernity. The decision on whether to have pale painted walls or more decorative wallpapered ones, or a particular design of furniture or curtains, was really a matter of taste and budget. The pared down 'modernist' interior, and the busier, more colourful suburban look are both very much part of the 1930s and there is much in between.

THIRTIESTYLE' reflects what was produced and marketed to middle-class consumers to decorate and furnish their homes. All its illustrations are taken from MoDA's collections of designs and trade catalogues, magazines and books published in the 1930s. It aims to inspire readers to be as enthusiastic about inter-war interiors as the owners of these dream homes were when they were first built.

WALLS AND PAINT

Wall decoration ranged from simple, plain, pale paint to complex arrangements of several papers with coordinating borders and decorative corners.

Painted walls created a simple clean space that was enlivened by patterned curtains, rugs and furniture. Walls and internal woodwork were often cream. Only pale coloured walls were felt to be suitable for the truly modern home. Walls usually had a matt finish. In very glamorous interiors gloss or varnished paint was chosen to complement furniture and curtains of shiny materials.

At the same time, wallpaper was sold in large quantities. Many homes decorated their walls with a single paper and a narrow border either under the picture rail or at ceiling level. Borders were also cut to create stepped patterns and to define areas of the wall where different papers were used. The more elaborate the border the simpler the main paper. Wallpaper 'corners' were fashionable and came in many designs, including geometric shapes and large cut-out trailing leaves and flowers.

Embossed 'porridge' papers added texture and were produced mainly in creams and dull colours. 'Autumn tints' - papers in shades of brown, orange, green and red - were very popular. Some hall papers had overall floral or leaf patterns.

Manufacturers produced 'companion' papers that worked well together and gave suggestions for their use. They encouraged people to customise their walls by creating individual schemes from the various papered elements on sale. Papering with such decorations was complicated and time-consuming. Professional decorators were often needed which added to the expense.

The buyers of new suburban homes usually had a limited choice of paint colours and wallpaper patterns, their selection being determined by those the developer offered. Woodwork was often grained, particularly where dark wooden furniture was used.

ILLUSTRATION I Painted in a pale colour, this simply furnished hallway demonstrates many key features of the elegant 1930s. In addition to its plain walls, note also the flush doors, single rug, spherical glass light, shiny curtain fabric and Finnish furniture. The radiator beneath the window indicates that this Victorian house has been updated with the latest technology.

ILLUSTRATION 2 This paint chart shows a range of pale matt colours, which were suitable for the walls of 1930s rooms. White, ivory, beige,

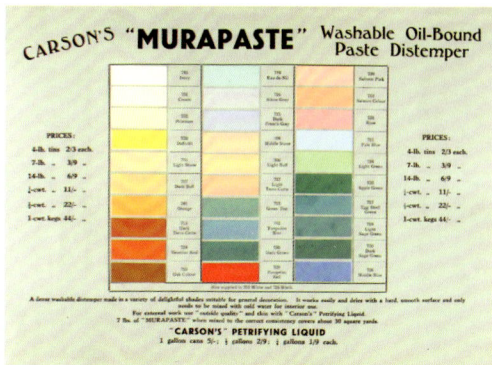

ILLUSTRATION 2
Carson's Paint Chart, 1939, Courtesy of Carson's

ILLUSTRATION 3
Champions Paint Chart, 1939, Courtesy of Champion's

ILLUSTRATION 4

Sanderson's Wallpaper
Pattern Book, 1933
Courtesy of MoDA

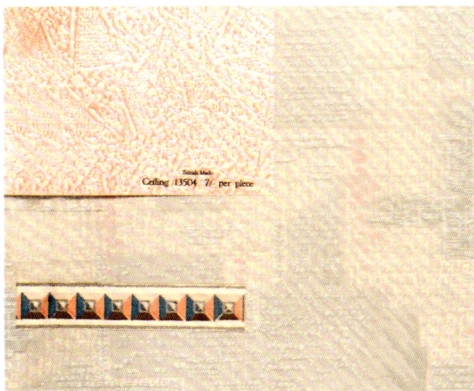

ILLUSTRATION 5

Sanderson's Wallpaper
Pattern Book, 1933
Courtesy of MoDA.

pale green, grey and pink were fashionable, in addition to cream. Some interiors used paints with a gloss or varnished finish, in keeping with shiny furniture and fabrics.

ILLUSTRATION 3 Deeper colours were available as gloss paint for woodwork, metal and stone. Exterior window frames and doors of suburban houses were often painted green. White and paler colours were used for modern flats and flat-roofed houses, both inside and out.

ILLUSTRATION 4 The 'Mayfair' bedroom decoration by the leading wallpaper manufacturer Arthur Sanderson & Sons combines a mottled pink ceiling paper with a predominantly grey wallpaper. The colour pink was used in bedrooms particularly.

ILLUSTRATION 5 Geometric wallpaper patterns were often used with plainish papers and narrow borders. Green was popular as were shades of brown and orange, known as 'Autumn tints'.

BADDA 558

ILLUSTRATION 6

Catalogue for T Whatley & Son, 1938
Courtesy of T. Whatley & Son.

ILLUSTRATION 6 The 'Pembroke Decoration', in a Middlesbrough decorator's catalogue, uses two main papers with a narrow border. The patterned filling paper contrasts with the main paper, which is a muted, 'porridge' paper. Manufacturers encouraged people to create their own individual wall decoration by combining plain and patterned papers in various ways.

ILLUSTRATION 7 Cut-out borders featuring leaves and flowers were popular. The 'Cactus' is described as having 'a hint of freakishness'. Many borders would have featured native plants.

ILLUSTRATION 8 These bedroom walls illustrate the use of a simple geometric corner and border scheme.

"Cactus"

Sheer delight in wallpaper decoration — where originality of motif comes without
a hint of freakishness. The decorative beauty of the Cactus Design is an inspiration
and an innovation as well! No small part of its distinction lies in the use of the
companion papers and the border to build up alternative schemes.

Lower Filling. 2900	... ...	6 - per piece
Upper Filling. 2901	... ...	4 6 per piece
21 inch Border. B.2901	... ...	3¾d. per yard
Pair of Subjects, respectively 17 ins. wide by 36 ins. high, and 36 ins. wide by 29½ ins.		
high. Ready cut out. (Only supplied in pairs.) B.2902	... ...	16 6 per pair
Green Mottled Ceiling Paper. 2903	... ...	3 6 per piece

ILLUSTRATION 7

Catalogue for T Whatley & Son, 1937

Courtesy of T. Whatley & Son.

ILLUSTRATION 8

Catalogue for WS Low, 1936

Courtesy of W. S. Low Ltd.

ILLUSTRATION 9

John Line and Sons' Wallpaper Pattern Book,
1934, Courtesy of John Line and Sons.

ILLUSTRATION 9 Narrow borders and 'corners' sold well. They were supplied separately and added to form a decorative frame on the wall. They were available in a range of patterns from 'Jazz' abstract to floral. The 'Crocus' shown here combines the two.

FLOORING

The 1930s was the decade of the rug. A huge variety of designs was available and a rug often formed the decorative focal point of a living room. Keeping the home clean and hygienic was a high priority and influenced many aspects of design for the home including flooring. Since a rug could be lifted for cleaning, unlike a fitted carpet, dust was less likely to get trapped. Rugs were therefore a good choice.

The 'chicest' homes included expensive hand-knotted rugs by leading designers such as Marion Dorn and Marian Pepler. These often featured abstract shapes and overlapping linear or geometric motifs in darker colours, such as brown, coral and blue, on a pale ground. Such rugs introduced a refined, elegant pattern to any room.

Rugs look best on a plain background. Ideally they were placed on light wooden boards, often of oak. In the suburbs the preference was usually to stain pine boards in a dark 'Jacobean' colour. Parquet oak floors were seen in hallways of more expensive homes.

Cheaper rugs were machine produced in large quantities to meet demand. While some had restrained patterns and colours, others had far bolder 'Jazz' designs. Oranges, greens and browns were often seen in rugs in suburban homes.

Despite the promotion of removable floor coverings as the easiest to keep clean, plain fitted carpets were an option for those who could afford them. In such homes there was likely to be a vacuum cleaner, making it possible to maintain a high standard of cleanliness. Dark brown was a favourite carpet colour and a rug would sit on it.

Larger patterned carpets were also widely available and many were made in bright, bold designs. For those who could not afford a carpet, patterned linoleum 'carpet squares' were a more economical option. Lino was, in any case, a practical choice for bedrooms, kitchens and bathrooms.

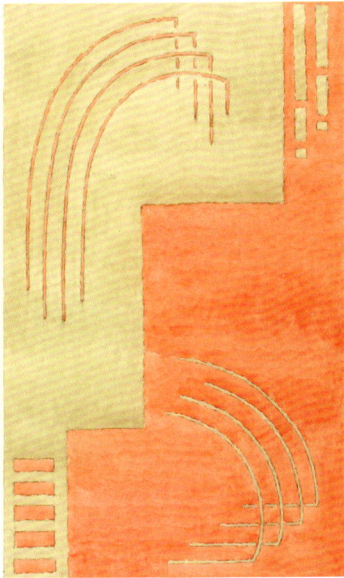

ILLUSTRATION 3

*Rug design by the Silver Studio, 1934,
Courtesy of MoDA.*

SD1504

ILLUSTRATION 1 As the focal point of a sitting room, the rug was placed between the fireplace and the seating. They were usually rectangular. The example is in stone, blue and chocolate brown. This three-piece suite is recommended for its adaptability; it can be arranged either to create a corner settee, as shown, or the pieces used separately.

ILLUSTRATION 2

Rug design by the Silver Studio, 1934, Courtesy of MoDA.

ILLUSTRATION 1

Catalogue for Bowman's, about 1939, Courtesy of Bowman Bros Ltd.

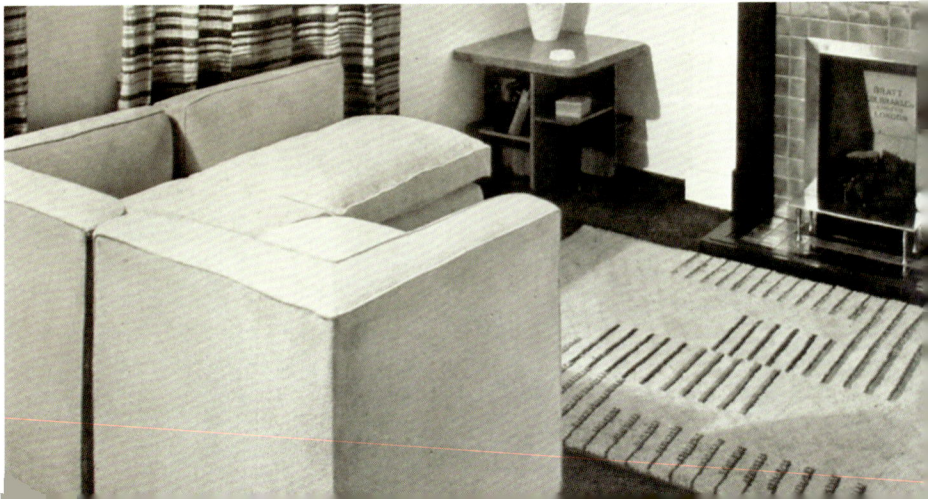

SD 471

ILLUSTRATION 4
The Ideal Home magazine, May 1935
© www.timeincukcontent.com

ILLUSTRATION 2 The elegant curved lines and contrasting light and dark halves of this design produce a clear, elegant pattern. It would have worked well with pale painted walls, and a glossy satin bedspread and cushions, to create a glamorous bedroom.

ILLUSTRATION 3 With its overlapping linear and geometric pattern and small areas of darker colours on a pale ground, this design would have been suitable for a smart interior scheme. It reflects the work of leading rug designers.

ILLUSTRATION 4 The blue and grey circular rug, with a pattern of concentric circles, is the most striking feature of this Surrey dining room with its cream, grey and blue colour scheme. The shape of the rug and table are similar. The rug sits on polished light oak boards, which form a neutral background.

BADDA 208

ILLUSTRATION 8

Catalogue for Bowman's, about 1935, Courtesy of Bowman Bros Ltd.

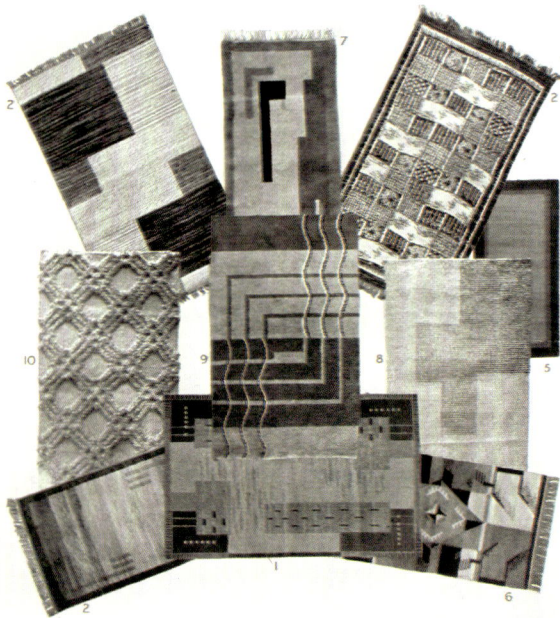

BADDA 179

1. Hair Cord Rug

2. Reversible Modern Wool Rug

5. Plain Axminster Rug

6. Hand-Woven Woollen Reversible Rug

7. Heavy Quality Hand-made Indian Rugs

8. Hand-made Axminster Rug

9. A Heavy Hand-made Axminster Rug

10. Part Tufted Rug

ILLUSTRATION 5 Carpets were available in many designs most of which were in browns, orange, beige and green. Such carpets were used in suburban homes where the wallpapers often had similar patterns.

ILLUSTRATION 6 This orange, red and brown 'Jazz' style design would have been suitable for use in front of the fire in a suburban home.

ILLUSTRATION 7 This carpet almost covers the entire floor. Its circular brown and blue pattern provides a bold decorative focus to the sitting room.

ILLUSTRATION 8 Rugs were available in every furniture store and there were a wide variety to choose from. Most designs were offered in a range of colours and some rugs were fringed. All these have abstract or geometric patterns but some are much plainer than others.

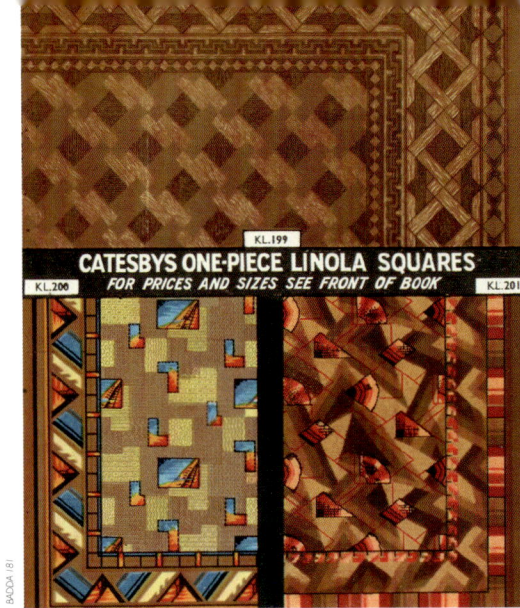

ILLUSTRATION 9
Catalogue for Catesby's, 1938, ©Catesbys.

BADDA 181

ILLUSTRATION 10
Catalogue for Catesby's, 1938, ©Catesbys.

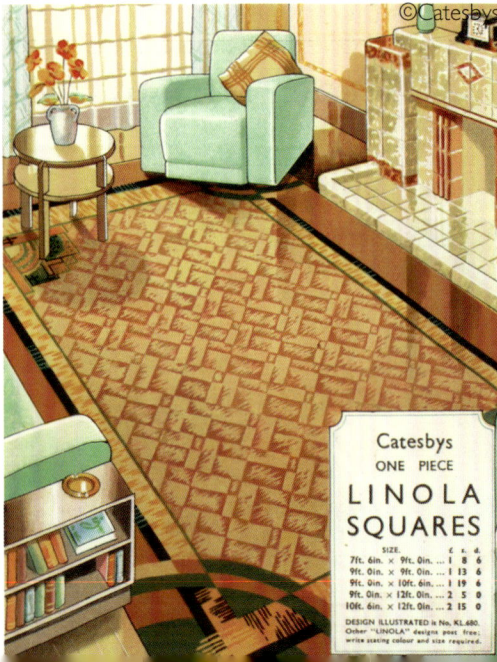

BADDA 181

ILLUSTRATION 9 Linoleum floor coverings were available in a wide range of patterns, some with 'Jazz' patterns, such as the bottom two examples. Plainer ones were also available. As with carpets, brown was a popular colour often combined with greens and oranges.

ILLUSTRATION 10 Linoleum 'rugs' or 'carpets' known as 'Linola Squares' were available too. As with woollen rugs, they were placed on a plain background, in this case on dark stained wooden floorboards. This rug covers most of the room but is still located in front of the fireplace, with the three-piece suite around it. Note the low bookcase up against the side of one armchair, which was a typical arrangement.

FURNITURE

New houses and flats were not as large as those built previously. Furniture was therefore smaller and less was needed to furnish a room. Built-in and multi-purpose furniture, such as tables with shelving, became available. 'Unit' furniture, which could be rearranged to suit different tastes and requirements, was also practical

Styles ranged from the 'traditional' to the 'modern'. The most avant-garde furniture was of bent wood or steel, inspired by designs from Continental Europe. This might, for example, be seen in city flats. At the other extreme, traditional dark wood suites were also widely available. They were often used in suburban homes.

Oak and exotic fruitwood veneers, such as cherry and walnut, were popular for the more traditional. Solid wood was rare due to the shortage of good timber. Jacobean-inspired furniture usually featured carving or moulding in dark oak. Plainer pieces made in light-coloured woods, such as sycamore or birch, were another option.

Finnish bent wood, birch furniture, such as that designed by Alvar Aalto, was very reasonably priced. Its flowing, modern shapes appealed to the avant-garde minority. Tubular steel furniture inspired by the Bauhaus and designers such as Mies van der Rohe was also available. The chairs had seats of canvas, leather or wood, and tabletops were made of wood or glass. Steel, along with other shiny materials, had an aura of glamour. By the mid-1930s people were mixing it with more traditional pieces.

Three-piece suites were important and desirable in living rooms. Often large, solid looking and square, they had fixed covers preferably in plain, woven fabrics. Low backs emphasised the horizontal lines of much furniture, including bookcases and cupboards. Small low tables were virtually indispensable pieces of occasional furniture.

The majority of dining-room tables were made of wood and they were sold in suites with matching upright chairs. Bedroom furniture also came in suites.

BADDA 179

ILLUSTRATION 1 Modern furniture was often designed to serve several functions. Smaller living spaces, such as the new flats designed to appeal to the urban middle classes, were one reason why multi-functional furniture became popular. So too was the general desire to avoid clutter in living spaces. In this 'bachelor flat', Bowman's, a large London furniture store, promotes its 'unit' furniture as flexible and adaptable.

ILLUSTRATION 2 This three-piece suite is low and broad with curved arms. Its shape and patterned upholstery are typical of more inexpensive furniture.

Nests of tables were a popular in living rooms. Brown and green was a typical colour scheme.

ILLUSTRATION 3 This living room display for the 1936 Ideal Home Exhibition shows modern style, light coloured furniture. It illustrates several key 1930s design features. Note the low, broad, square three-piece suite upholstered in a plain, woven fabric. The nest of tables, occasional table and shelving are also low emphasising the horizontal. The rug is a prominent decorative feature introducing a strong patterned element to the room.

BADDA 53

ILLUSTRATION 4 Finnish steam-bent, plywood birch furniture is simple and utilitarian in complete contrast to more traditional dark, carved furniture. It attracted much attention in the design press and appealed to the avant-garde buyer. Alvar Aalto designed this chair and tea table. The table's legs, and chair's back and arms, are curved and the furniture is light in colour and weight.

ILLUSTRATION 5 Many of the dining suites on sale were in a Jacobean style. Made from oak, they were

BADDA 178

ILLUSTRATION 6
Catalogue for Arding & Hobbs, 1937, © Debenhams.

ILLUSTRATION 7
Beautiful home, Arding & Hobbs Ltd, Clapham Junction, London, catalogue, 1937, © Debenhams.

dark and heavy with carved legs. Big sideboards were common and took up considerable space. This dining suite has a matching extending dining table and four chairs covered in hide.

ILLUSTRATION 6 Oak dining room furniture in a 'modern' style was on sale. Its size made it suitable for homes where space was limited and which might have a combined sitting and dining room. This sideboard is plainer and smaller than Jacobean-inspired furniture, but still includes some decorative elements, such as a carved front.

ILLUSTRATION 7 Bedrooms often had a more luxurious and feminine feeling than other rooms, sometimes featuring exotic wood veneers and shiny surfaces. This walnut veneered bedroom suite with its rounded corners and feet is Art Deco-inspired. The bedside cupboard includes a practical bookshelf enabling it to serve more than one function in the room.

ILLUSTRATION 8

Catalogue for Bowman's, about 1935, Courtesy of Bowman Bros Ltd.

ILLUSTRATION 8 Modern style furniture was produced in light-coloured woods, such as sycamore. It was sometimes combined with a darker wood, like mahogany, used here as an edging. This bedroom suite is angular and low. The wardrobe is made up of three units at two different heights, which can be placed in various arrangements. Chrome steel tubular furniture, like this armchair, was widely available by the mid-1930s and was used to add glamour to interiors.

CURTAINS, CUSHIONS AND UPHOLSTERY

Fabrics were typically used to introduce pattern and texture into otherwise plain schemes.

Curtains hung from the floor to the ceiling from a rail. Often there was a plain square pelmet, either painted to match the walls or covered in fabric. When drawn, the curtains created a large area of pattern and colour, with a rug providing the only other decorative focus of a room. Designs ranged from simple abstracts to florals and brightly coloured geometric patterns.

Upholstery fabrics were mainly woven and often patterned. But in the most avant-garde homes covers were plainer, often of textured woven fabric, more in keeping with the clean square shape of the chairs and settees.

Shiny fabrics also had their place. Satin was particularly popular for bedrooms where curtains, quilted bedspreads and cushions would all help to create a luxurious environment. In some glamorous interiors, the newly introduced artificial silks and satins complemented the shiny walls and furniture. Curtains might be made of a printed satin and the cushions covered in a plain satin.

In the 1930s, patterns for both printed and woven textiles featured abstract forms and geometric shapes. Stripes, triangles, squares and curves all occurred, creating a more restrained form of pattern than seen previously. These up-to-date patterns worked well with plainer, light wood furniture and painted walls. The most expensive were by well-known designers and artists and were silk-screen printed by hand.

More traditional patterns were also popular but even these frequently contained modern elements. Flowers and geometric shapes often featured on less expensive fabrics, often in bright colours. For those who preferred historic styles of furnishing, there were plenty of Jacobean-inspired fabrics derived from sixteenth and seventeenth century embroideries.

ILLUSTRATION I Set against stone coloured painted walls, the curtains are the most prominent decorative feature of this North London sitting room. With a fashionable abstract pattern, hand printed on linen in terracotta, dark blue and beige, they are particularly striking when drawn. The pale slate and dull brown hand tufted rug, on the oak polished floor, gives another point of interest. The chairs, by contrast, are covered in a plain textured fabric.

ILLUSTRATION 2 This luxurious bedroom has a satin down quilt, bedspread and cushion. The room has an altogether shiny feel. The pink striped wallpaper has a glossy finish. The curtains, made from printed satin by Allan Walton, a leading fabric retailer, are in a fashionable abstract pattern. Note the plain wooden pelmet, which has been painted to match the pink walls.

ST 32

ILLUSTRATION 3

Textile designed by the Silver Studio, 1935 ,
Courtesy of MoDA.

BADDA 953

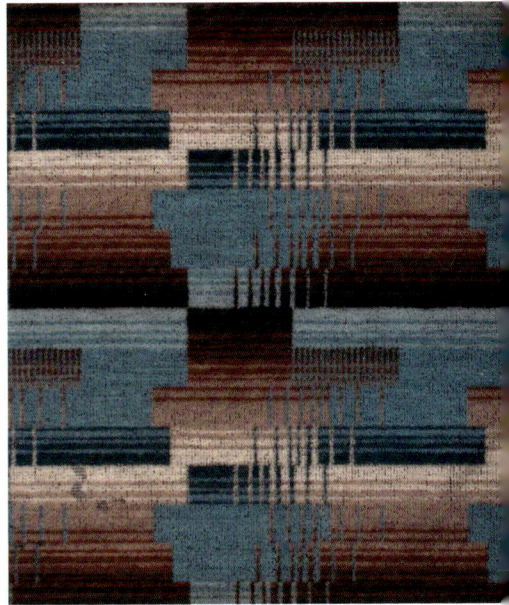

ILLUSTRATION 3 Woven fabrics
with geometric patterns, and in
muted colours like green, brown
and beige, were popular for
upholstery. Texture was also often
a feature. Fabrics such as this, in
which threads have been cut during
manufacture to create a pile, were
known as 'moquettes'.

ILLUSTRATION 2

Modern Furnishing and Decoration by Derek Patmore, 1936 ,
Courtesy of The Studio Limited.

ILLUSTRATION 4
Textile designed by the Silver Studio, about 1935,
Courtesy of MoDA.

ILLUSTRATION 4 In many suburban homes three-piece suites were upholstered in fabrics like this that combined geometric shapes with floral motifs. Brown and green often featured, frequently combined with orange. **ILLUSTRATION 5** This attractive woven textile might have been used in a suburban home.

The wave pattern ran horizontally along the back of a sofa or armchair. **ILLUSTRATION 6** Brightly coloured textiles like this show the influence of Art Deco colours and patterns. Inexpensive printed cotton fabrics with patterns of swerving lines and stylised flowers were used for curtains in a large number of 1930s homes.

ILLUSTRATION 5
Textile, about 1939, Courtesy of MoDA.

ILLUSTRATION 7

Textile designed by the Silver Studio, about 1935
Courtesy of MoDA.

ILLUSTRATION 7 'Shadow tissue' or warp printed textiles were suitable for curtains. Through a combination of printing and weaving, colours are combined to create a soft, slightly 'out of focus' effect. Florals never entirely disappeared from fabrics for the home and such traditional imagery was often combined with more modern abstract forms.

ILLUSTRATION 8 Linen printed fabrics created a 'natural' surface, in contrast to the shiny fabrics that were often used in rooms with modern chrome furniture. A pattern like this introduced a strong decorative element to a room, particularly as curtains hung straight from a rail at ceiling height to the floor.

ILLUSTRATION 9 Printed on linen, this fabric would work well with pale painted walls. The inclusion of stylised cloud shapes makes it more suited to a smart suburban house than an avant-garde interior.

ST 224

ILLUSTRATION 9

Textile designed by the Silver Studio, about 1935, Courtesy of MoDA.

ST 232

ILLUSTRATION 10

Catalogue for Liberty's, Spring 1936
© Liberty.

LIBERTY
PRINTED LINENS
(FAST COLOURS)

For Loose Covers and Curtains

(105) Range No. 2701 to 2705 (as illustrated). A charming Jacobean design printed in five delightful colour schemes of red, orange, wine, blue, and orange and blue.

30 ins. wide. 4 6 a yard.

Others from 2 6 a yard.

PATTERNS SENT ON REQUEST
Skilled representatives sent, free of charge, to advise on all details connected with curtains and loose covers.

ILLUSTRATION 10 Historic 'Jacobean' designs continued to be produced alongside contemporary abstract patterns. They appealed to the more traditional homemaker, as did Jacobean-inspired furniture, and were used for curtains and occasionally to cover chairs. This Liberty's linen is typical and a range of manufacturers produced similar fabrics.

FIREPLACES AND HEATING

Fireplaces were an important feature of most 1930s homes. They were located centrally on one wall providing a focal point in the living room and seating was arranged around them. Low shelving or cupboards might extend to each side maximising the use of space. A rug was essential in front of the fireplace, often with an abstract pattern.

Heating could be generated by coal, gas or electricity. The choice depended on your location, ideas and budget. Tiled stepped fireplaces were frequently to be found in new suburban houses. Tiling was often plain with perhaps some simple geometric patterns and there might be a wooden mantelpiece. Low, horizontal marble fireplaces and shiny built-in and portable electric fires were other options.

In some suburban houses the fire in the dining room, the main family living space, was kept alight constantly all year round. Kitchens were small and there was not always space to fit an independent boiler. In this case hot water was provided by a back boiler installed in the fire.

Small, portable electric fires were useful where immediate heat was needed. They were often found in rooms that were used for only part of the day, like bedrooms.

The most modern energy source was electricity but this was expensive and few sockets were fitted in homes. Modern flats were particularly well equipped and many gave tenants a choice of energy for heating. Most included a chimneybreast into which a shiny gas or electric bar fire was fitted. Such heating was clean and modern.

Wall mounted central-heating radiators were new and offered another efficient method of heating but they were expensive to run. They were found mostly in urban flats but the living room would still feature a fireplace.

ILLUSTRATION 1

Catalogue for Candy & Co, about 1935
Courtesy of Candy and Company Limited.

BADDA 332

BADDA 268

☛ SMART CURB SUITE in
GREEN & CHROMIUM

A.H. 1634

CURB	37/-
COMPANION	35/-
SCREEN	25/-
COAL BOX	39/-
SUITE	136/-

This delightful and most attractive Curb Suite is strongly made and well finished throughout. It will give lasting and efficient service. Very special value.

DAINTY CURB SUITE ☛

A.H. 1674	Chromium Plated	Antique Copper	Oxidised Silver
CURB	34/-	34/-	48/-
COMPANION	19/6	10/-	18/-
SCREEN	36/-	36/-	48/-
COAL BOX	42/-	42/-	54/-
SUITE	131/6	122/-	168/-

☛ HANDSOME CURB SUITE

CURB	46/-	40/-	44/-	58/-
COMPANION	21/-	19/-	21/-	30/-
SCREEN	33/-	30/-	33/-	44/-
COAL BOX	43/-	40/-	44/-	58/-
SUITE	143/-	129/-	142/-	190/-

A FINE CURB SUITE

A.H. 4823	Chromium Plated	Antique Copper	Oxidised Silver
CURB	45/-	45/-	54/-
COMPANION	31/6	22/6	27/-
SCREEN	36/-	36/-	48/-
COAL BOX	42/-	42/-	54/-
SUITE	154/6	145/6	183/-

☛ A MODERN SEAT CURB

A.H. 1642 This elegant Curb has a Cellulose sprayed base in colours of Green, Blue, Orange, Black, etc. Furnished with Chromium-plated steel tubes and Rexine seats.
Size overall, 14in. by 12in. by 18in. high.

£4.7.0

ARDING & HOBBS LTD., CLAPHAM JUNCTION, LONDON, S.W.11

BADDA 783

ILLUSTRATION 1 Tiled fireplaces, many with stepped shapes, were widely available. Supplied in pre-formed sections they were easy to fit. In living rooms they were normally for coal fires. Beige, brown or blue tiles were most common. Some included simple geometric patterns by adding a second and even a third colour tile. Dark wooden mantelpieces were sometimes added. There was often a mirror above the fireplace.

ILLUSTRATION 2 Metal curbs, fireguards, coal boxes and other fire accessories were produced in a range of designs for suburban houses with coal fires. Some had stepped patterns reflecting fire shapes.

ILLUSTRATION 3 Shiny marble fireplaces were available. This 'Heaped' fire is low and broad with tiered curves on each side. Steel inserts create a horizontally banded pattern.

BADDA 783

BADDA 953

ILLUSTRATION 4

Catalogue for Bratt Colbran, about 1935,
Courtesty of Bratt Colbran.

ILLUSTRATION 4 Some fireplaces were designed for use with more than one fuel. This 'Solectra radiator' could be fitted for coal or electricity. Its surround is made from marble and its shape emphasises the horizontal low lines of the interior.

ILLUSTRATION 5

Modern Furnishing and Decoration by
Derek Patmore, 1936
Courtesy of The Studio Limited.

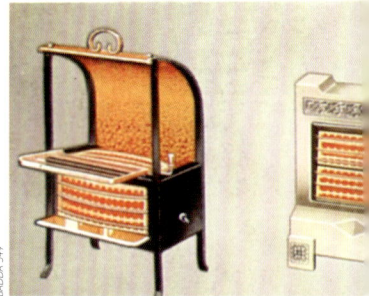

BADDA 549

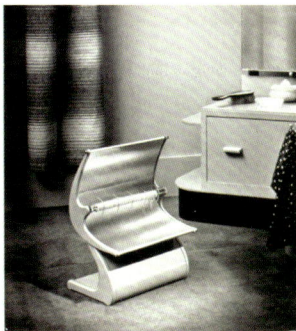

SOLECTRA RADIATORS

BRATT COLBRAN LIMITED, 10 Mortimer Street, London, W.1.
TELEPHONES   MUSEUM 9431 & 9311   10 LINES

ILLUSTRATION 5 The Ferranti electric fire is an iconic 1930s design. Fitting flush into the fire surround, its shiny chrome parabolic reflector gives it great visual impact as well as helping it to diffuse heat efficiently. Here the fire is the central focus of the room.

ILLUSTRATION 6 Electric portable fires were another useful source of heating particularly in bedrooms. Providing instant heat, they could be used for short periods, unlike coal fires. They were often styled to reflect the modernity, efficiency and convenience of the product. Parabolic reflector fires, such as this 'Flamingo' model, looked particularly modern.

ILLUSTRATION 7 Not all electric fires had shiny metal surfaces. Some even had coal and flame effects to mimic coal fires. Creda produced fires in a range of coloured finishes as well as traditional designs of black and copper.

ILLUSTRATION 6
Catalogue for Bratt Colbran, about 1935
Courtesy of Bratt Colbran.

ILLUSTRATION 7
Catalogue for Creda, 1938-1939
Courtesy of Simplex Electric Company Limited.

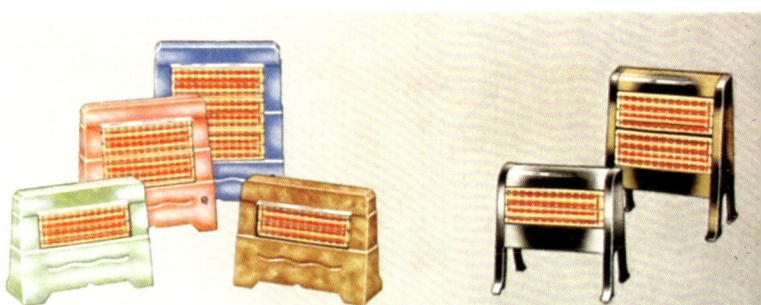

THE FOUR COLUMN

A radiator of strikingly graceful lines yet of sound and sturdy construction withal. When wall space and floor area call for a radiator neither too long nor too wide, the right amount of heating surface is often best supplied by the Four-column ''Pall Mall'' Radiator.

BADDA 490

FOR WATER OR STEAM

Four-column radiators can be supplied with 6" legs. Prices on page 20.

ILLUSTRATION 8
Catalogue for Crane Radiators, 1933
Courtesy of Crane Radiators

ILLUSTRATION 9
Cata Illustration 8

Catalogue for Bratt Colbran, about 1935 , Courtesy of Bratt Colbran.

BADDA 783

ILLUSTRATION 8 Radiators as part of a central-heating system were still unusual and expensive. They were rarely seen in suburban houses. This four column 'Pall Mall' radiator would have been suitable for heating large spaces, such as living rooms. Narrower two column radiators were available for use in bedrooms and corridors.

ILLUSTRATION 9 Flush panel gas or electric fires could be fitted into the fireplace opening but this 'Portcullis' gas fire, with its light green Swedish marble surround, is set flush into the wall. A shelf above forms a mantelpiece.

L 8742

FARNHAM
*
Ref. Nos. L 8742, 12 in
L 8743, 14 in   L 8744, 16 in
Prices as table below

L 8745

L 8748

FERMOY
Ref. Nos. L 8745, 12 in
L 8746, 14 in L 8747, 16 in
Prices as table below

FERNAN
Ref. Nos. L 8748, 12 in
L 8749, 14 in L 8750, 16 in
Prices as table below

Diam.	Lamp recom-mended	PRICE EACH		
		Polished Brass	Oxidised Copper	Oxidised Silver
In	Watts	£ s d	£ s d	£ s d
12	75	1 16 6	1 18 0	1 19 0
14	100	2 10 0	2 11 6	2 12 6
16	150	3 6 6	3 8 0	3 9 0

Prices include Holders, but not Wiring or Lamps

BADDA 594

ILLUSTRATION 4

*Catalogue for The Sun Electrical Company, 1931
Courtesy of The Sun Electrical Company Limited.*

L 8348
ARAGON
Constructed of brass and
glazed with plain obscured
glass
Width 6 in

L 8348 Antique Brass
£1 2 3 each
L 8349 Oxidised Copper
£1 4 6 each
L 8350 Oxidised Silver
£1 8 0 each

L 8345
ARADA
Constructed of brass and
glazed with muffled glass
Width 6 in
L 8345 Antique Brass
£1 9 0 each
L 8346 Oxidised Copper
£1 12 0 each
L 8347 Oxidised Silver
£1 16 0 each

L 8351
ARAKAN
Constructed of brass and
glazed with muffled glass
4½ in square
L 8351 Antique Brass
£1 7 6 each
L 8352 Oxidised Copper
£1 10 0 each
L 8353 Oxidised Silver
£1 14 6 each

*Prices include Holders, but not Wiring or Lamps
Lamps recommended, 60 watt Gasfilled*

BADDA 594

ILLUSTRATION 5

*Catalogue for The Sun Electrical Company, 1931
Courtesy of The Sun Electrical Company Limited.*

ILLUSTRATION 3 Glass shades were available in a wide range of designs. Small glass 'alabaster' shades had been sold since the 1920s. They came in a range of colours and were tinted permanently to imitate alabaster. These pink shades were designed for bedrooms.

ILLUSTRATION 4 'Alabaster' bowl pendants were found in the living rooms of many suburban houses. They hung from three long chains and varied bowl shapes were available, as well as different coloured 'alabaster' effects.

ILLUSTRATION 5 Lantern lights were intended for hallways and hung from a single brass chain. These lanterns are made of brass and glass and were typically purchased for suburban houses.

ILLUSTRATION 6 Standard lamps with metallic uplighters provided soft, well-diffused light in rooms with shiny materials. This one was offered in three finishes, chrome, bronze and copper.

PENDANT
A.H. 1599. A handsome and attractive design with chromium-plated metal work and satin-finished glass shades. Spread overall, 15in.
£3.12.0

AN ATTRACTIVE PENDANT
A.H. 1597. Chromium-plated metal work. Satin-finished glass shades. With shades, wired complete. Spread overall 16in.
£5.12.0

Visit our Electrical Department, Lower Ground Floor, and see the extensive variety of fittings.

A DAINTY PENDANT
A.H. 1589. Ivory and Green (or any cellulose colour), shades tinted to match. With shades and holders, wired complete.
£4.15.6

PENDANT
A.H. 1598. Chromium-plated metal work and satin-finished shades. With shades, wired complete. Spread overall, 17½in.
£4.3.6

"BELISHA BEACON" STANDARD
A.H. 1111. Black, with Chromium-plated bands. Wired 5yd. flex. Shade carrier, push bar, lamp-holder and plug.
£3.5.0

A.H. 252. PARCHMENT and MOIRE "BEACON" SHADE. Silk thonged. Trimmed 6in. silk fringe.
£2.5.0

FLOOR STANDARD
A.H. 30. Chromium plated. Wired with 5yd. flex. Shade carrier, push bar, holder and plug.
£2.17.0

A.H. 236. PARCHMENT and RHODELINE SHADE. Silk thonged and trimmed 6in. silk fringe.
£1.9.0

FLOOR STANDARD
A.H. 1116. Chromium plated. Wired 5yd. flex. Shade carrier, push bar, lampholder and plug.
£2.12.0

A.H. 239. MOIRE and RHODE-LINE SHADE. Silk thonged and trimmed 6in. silk fringe. Any colours.
£2.13.0

FLOOR STANDARD
A.H. 2 Wood base and stem sprayed Black or Green cellulose. Fitted chromium-plated metal bands. Wired 5yd. flex. Shade carrier, push bar, lamp-holder and plug.
£2.12.6

A.H. 222 PARCHMENT and RHODE-LINE SHADE Silk thonged and finished 6in. silk tassels.
£1.9.6

"EAGLE" LAMP
Chromium plated. Triangular base, 8in. by 8in. by 8in. Height, 12½in. Glass globe, 8⅜in. diameter. Pale Green, Pale Amber, Pale Pink, or Opal.
85/-

"EGYPTIAN CORNER"
Modern style Lamp. Chromium plated. Wired silk-covered flex, switch and adaptor. Triangular base, 6½in. by 4½in. Height of metal work, 5½in.
32/-

"METEOR"
Chromium plated Triangular base, 8in. by 8in. by 8in. Height, 14½in. Glass globe, 8⅜in. diameter. In Pale Green, Pale Amber, Pale Pink, or Opal.
85/-

The 'CRESCENT' TABLE LAMP
Chromium plated. Wired. Complete with silk-covered flex, switch and adaptor. Triangular base, 6½in. by 4½in. Height by 4½in. Height, 12½in.
37/-

ARDING & HOBBS LTD., CLAPHAM JUNCTION, LONDON, S.W.11

ILLUSTRATION 8
Catalogue for Arding & Hobbs, 1937
© Debenhams.

ILLUSTRATION 7
Catalogue for Gardiner Sons, 1936
© Gardiner Sons & Co Ltd.

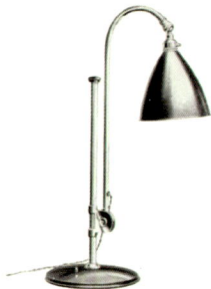

ILLUSTRATION 7 Adjustable metal table lamps included 'Bestlites' and 'Anglepoise' lamps. Used on desks and bedside tables, they could be altered as needed to light specific areas for reading and work. Similar metal standard lamps were also on sale. This chrome and black 'Bestlite' was popular and highly practical.

ILLUSTRATION 8 A huge variety of lights were on sale. Standard floor lamps with fringed shades, some with geometric patterns, were often placed near chairs for reading. Triple pendant lights with uplighter glass shades were for central ceiling lights. Table lights, including some with figures, were for low surfaces.

FINISHING TOUCHES

Decorative objects and fixtures ranged from simply shaped pieces with limited decoration to those featuring brightly coloured surface decoration.

At one extreme, some rooms had only a few, carefully positioned pieces, such as an animal figurine on the mantelshelf, a single painting above and perhaps one vase of flowers. Arrangements were usually of one type of flower, often lilies or chrysanthemums with no additional greenery. In this sort of scheme single colours and streamlined shapes were often chosen. Pattern was confined to ribbing, simple geometric patterns and coloured bands.

Other homemakers preferred more obviously decorative objects. Brightly coloured ceramics and glass were very popular. Surface patterns of stylised flowers and geometric shapes in orange, yellow, black and blue sold well. Pieces by Clarice Cliff and Susie Cooper were widely available. Even in rooms where such colourful pieces were used, there would still be far fewer objects than in a turn-of-the-century home. Walls were generally left bare or with few pictures, and surfaces were relatively empty.

Wireless radios were widespread by the mid-1930s. For many people, a radio was one of the first electric appliances they purchased and it was meant to be admired. The whole family would gather round to listen. Early models looked like traditional wooden cabinet furniture but many later examples were smaller, designed to be placed on shelves or sideboards. Some were made in streamlined shapes in Bakelite, a new plastic

There were many moulded Bakelite goods for the home, fulfilling various functions. As well as door handles, desk sets and kitchen equipment, there were Bakelite clocks and telephones. The telephone was still relatively novel but was becoming an essential item in the well-to-do middle-class home.

ILLUSTRATION 3
Catalogue for Bowman's, about 1935
Courtesy of Bowman Bros Ltd.

MODERN CLOCKS

Eight-day movements in Chromium
Plate and Glass — in a variety of colours

Luminous Dial. Height 3½ inches · £2 . 15 . 0

Height 5 inches · · · £5 . 0 . 0

Height 5 inches · · £10 . 10 . 0

AN ILLUSTRATED CATALOGUE OF MODERN CLOCKS
WILL BE GLADLY SENT UPON APPLICATION

**THE GOLDSMITHS
& SILVERSMITHS
COMPANY · LTD**
112 REGENT ST · LONDON · W1
AT THE CORNER OF GLASSHOUSE STREET—NO OTHER ADDRESS

ILLUSTRATION 2
The Ideal Home magazine, September 1935
© www.timeinukcontent.com.

ILLUSTRATION 1 The dining table in this architect-designed house is set with plain, undecorated plates and crockery and simple cutlery. The glass tumblers and jug are in a chequered pattern. A bowl of glass balls is used as the table centrepiece.

ILLUSTRATION 2 In suburban homes, clocks were sometimes placed on shelves or above the fireplace. They were available in various shapes and finishes including chrome and glass.

ILLUSTRATION 3 Table glass was uncut and sometimes coloured, as in these glasses with their black bases and a simple banded shape. Cocktails were fashionable and cocktail glasses and cabinets were found in many homes.

ILLUSTRATION 4 Susie Cooper tableware sold well. The Kestrel shape coffee set with its simple banded pattern is a typical design. There are lots of shiny surfaces in this black, chromium and glass tea trolley.

ILLUSTRATION 4
Catalogue for Bowman's, about 1939
Courtesy of Bowman Bros Ltd.

*T*HE Gloria Con
sole is the de luxe
Ferranti instrument o:
the year. It is a super-
het with the new
" electric " tuning
automatic volume con
trol and a tone control
The price is 29 guinea

ILLUSTRATION 5 Wedgwood vases and bowls designed by Keith Murray were much advertised. They came in bold, new shapes emphasized by distinctive ribbing and in various plain matt glazes. Wedgwood animal figurines were popular items above the fireplace or on the top of low shelves. John Skeaping designed this 'Standing Duiker'.

LATEST DESIGN
Attractive frameless mirror with modern decoration in selected Oak. Size, 26in. by 18in.
PRICE £1.1.6

Have your mirrors re-silvered. Esti-mates given Free.

See our specimen Furnished Rooms on the Second Floor.

A.H. 1047 **FRAMELESS MIRROR**
Charming modern design suitable for dining- or drawing-room. Enriched with Chro-mium-plated decoration. Size, 29in. by 19in.
PRICE £1.7.6

A.H. 1043 **OF NOVEL DESIGN**
An ornate frameless bevelled mirror with Chromium-plated decoration and chain. Will enhance any modern furnishing scheme. Size, 26in. by 16in.
PRICE 17'6

A.H. 1044 **FRAMELESS MIRROR**
A distinguished piece which will lend dignity and charm to the drawing or dining-room. Enriched with Chromium-plated ornaments and chain. Size, 27in. by 16in.
PRICE £1.3.6

A.H. 1042 **SIMPLE DESIGN**
A good quality Mirror of unobtrusive elegance, framed in either Mahogany or Walnut. Size, 31in. by 19in. to outside edges.
PRICE £2.5.0

UNIQUE STYLE
An artistic frameless mirror, well suited to modern fur-nishing schemes, the chain and neat decoration being of Chromium. Size, 27in. by 16in.
PRICE £1.3.6

A.H. 1046 **WALNUT FRAME**
Tasteful mirror in bevelled plate-glass with frame in a cross-banded design, with hand-some enrichments. Size, 29in. by 19in.
PRICE £1.19.6

A.H. 1048 **OVAL MIRROR**
A charming exponent of the oval style with fancy bevelled edge. A popular choice where simplicity is appreciated. Size, 29in. by 19in.
PRICE £1.4.6
Size, 26in. by 16in. **PRICE** 17/6

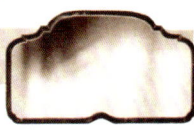

A.H. 1045 **WALNUT FRAME**
A novel and artistic plain plate mirror with frame of best selected Walnut. Equally suitable for bedroom or dining-room. Size, 16in. by 28in.
PRICE £1.15.6

ARDING & HOBBS LTD., CLAPHAM JUNCTION, LONDON, S.W.11

ILLUSTRATION 7
Catalogue for Arding & Hobbs, 1937
© Debenhams.

ILLUSTRATION 6 Most homes had a radio by the mid-1930s. It would be placed at the heart of the living room in a suburban house and brought news of the wider world into the home for many families. Originally radios were designed to look like pieces of furniture and were enclosed in wooden cases. Later smaller, table-top models were produced in either a wood or a streamlined Bakelite case. This deluxe Ferranti example is styled to look like a piece of furniture.

ILLUSTRATION 7 Mirrors were often placed above a fireplace in a suburban house. They were generally frameless and hung from a chain. Many geometric shapes were available, some with stepped tops.

ILLUSTRATION 8 Brush sets for men and women were available for dressing tables. This lady's set consists of two hairbrushes and a comb, a hand mirror plus a hat and a clothes brush. It was available in blue, green or yellow. Its luxurious feel suits the bedroom.

6-Piece Brush Set

	Any piece sold
Best quality London-made. Extra heavy quality. separately. (PS 5742). *Obtainable in all Colours.*	
Hand Mirror (11 × 4 ins.)	5 12 6
2 Hair Brushes, each £3 10 0	7 0 0
Hat Brush	1 12 6
Cloth Brush	1 12 6
Comb. Silver Gilt Mount	1 12 6
Set of Six Pieces	**£16 10 0**
Price in Plush £17 10 0	

ILLUSTRATION 8
Catalogue for Harrods, 1932
Courtesy of Harrods

ILLUSTRATION 9

Catalogue for Gardiner Sons, 1936

©Gardiner Sons & Co Ltd

ILLUSTRATION 9 Most 1930s homes included some Bakelite, a new type of plastic, which could be moulded into many shapes and produced in a range of colours. As well as telephones, radios, clocks and kitchen accessories, there were Bakelite door handles and lock sets. Angular, step-shaped sets were popular for the interior doors of suburban homes. Many, like these, were made in a brown imitation walnut.

ILLUSTRATION 10 Shiny metal lever handles and locks with streamlined styling were recommended for urban flats.

ILLUSTRATION 10

The Flat Book by J.L. Martin and S. Speight, 1939, © ColArt.

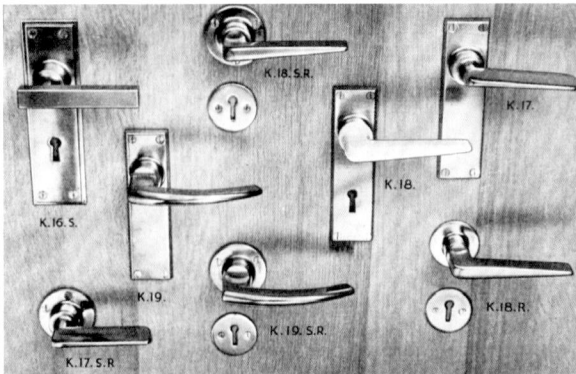

KITCHENS

With domestic help now scarce, much attention was paid to kitchen design in middle class homes. Lightness, cleanliness and convenience were important in creating a bright, efficient room. Great thought was given to the relationship between the sink, cooker and food preparation areas to minimise unnecessary movement.

Hygiene was a particularly important aspect of kitchen design. Cupboard doors were always smooth rather than panelled, as they were easier to clean. Similar concerns meant that plain or patterned linoleum was often used on kitchen floors, although some floors were tiled. Walls were painted with pale washable paint. Cupboards replaced open-shelved dressers. Both fitted units and freestanding wooden cabinets, which included many useful storage units and built-in equipment, such as a sieve, were on sale.

Many sinks were large and square, made of white ceramic, but stainless steel was also becoming available. There would be a draining board to one or both sides.

Kitchens were relatively small and the use of space had to be maximised. Many ingenious features such as pull-out work surfaces, ironing boards and tables were developed. Families might eat in the kitchen, but guests would be entertained in a separate dining room and serving hatches were often located between these two rooms.

The increased availability of electricity in the home allowed the development of a wide range of new kitchen appliances. Electric irons were popular and electric toasters were found in a number of homes. Gas and electricity offered alternative new methods of cooking. Freestanding stoves were convenient, especially if they had the newly introduced thermostat. Traditional solid-fuel ranges were still available too. More people cooked with gas than electricity. Gas also powered more refrigerators. However, most homes relied on a cool larder off the kitchen for food storage; fridges were still too expensive for most people.

ILLUSTRATION 1

Flats - Municipal and Private Enterprise
by Ascot Gas Water Heaters, 1938
Courtesy of Ascot Gas Water Heaters

ILLUSTRATION 1 In this well-equipped kitchen the distance between the food preparation surfaces, the cooker and the sink have been minimised and unnecessary decoration eliminated. It has built-in cupboards and shelves, and a slot-in 'streamline' electric cooker. A gas water heater is located under the work surface, near the washing area. Note also the plain linoleum floor covering and geometric patterned rug. Designed as a model kitchen for a working class flat, it was exhibited in Glasgow in 1938.

However few such kitchens existed in working class homes.

ILLUSTRATION 2 This modern kitchen was fitted in some of the new inter-war houses built in the suburbs by Laing. Many features were designed to be 'pulled-out' and 'put-way' to maximise the use of space. The table is shown extended for family meals. It also includes a fold-out double seat and ironing board.

ILLUSTRATION 2

Catalogue for Laing, 1935

Courtesy of John Laing & Son Limited

LAINGS · DE LUXE · KITCHEN

This photograph shows a corner of one of the 'De Luxe' Kitchens. In the Jubilee House and in several types of houses in Laing Estates. Therein is seen the ultra modern Cabinet which has so many attractive features which satisfy the most modern of housewives and dispel for ever the old idea that there is no pleasure in the kitchen—a pull-out table with folding double seat at one side, taking its food warm but instantly available for meals, a roll-away ironing board, ample cupboard for china, a sensible ventilated larder, cutlery drawer, cupboards for stores and many other wonderful notions. In addition, the kitchen has a gas copper, hot water boiler, draining boards to deep sink, and a red tiled floor. The room is well lighted and has a tiled recess for gas stove.

ILLUSTRATION 3 This ultra modern kitchen was designed for a London flat by the architectural practice, Tecton. It includes many cupboards for storage; one has a roller shutter front and pull-out tabletop. The inclusion of an electric fridge and a stainless steel sink are other notable features.

ILLUSTRATION 4 This small kitchen, designed by the architect Wells Coates, has a large, square white ceramic sink located between the cooker and gas fridge, and lots of adjacent food storage cupboards. The wall cabinet includes a built-in flour sieve and there is a wooden, wall-mounted plate rack. Washable paint has been used on the walls.

ILLUSTRATION 3

The Flat Book by J.L. Martin and S. Speight, 1939

© *Architectural Press Archive / RIBA Library Photographs Collection.*

ILLUSTRATION 4

The Flat Book by J.L. Martin and S. Speight, 1939

Courtesy of The Shenval Press.

BADDA 1413

Catalogue for Ostens, about 1935, Courtesy of Ostens.

ILLUSTRATION 6
Catalogue for Gardiner Sons, 1936
© Gardiner Sons & Co Ltd.

BADDA 855

ILLUSTRATION 5 Meals were served to guests in the dining room. A hatch between the kitchen and dining room was a practical feature of many larger suburban houses. Its introduction in the 1930s into middle class homes followed the disappearance of domestic help other than for the very rich. A housewife was expected to cook dinner and still be an excellent hostess.

ILLUSTRATION 6 Freestanding wooden cabinets fitted with many useful storage units had been introduced in the 1920s. Many were in natural pine but in architect-designed kitchens they often had a white finish. In addition to shelves and cutlery drawers, they contained places to store eggs and flour, and even a built-in sieve. A pull-out enamel work surface was included and plenty of glass jars for storing provisions. Some even came with suggested shopping lists and meal plans to help the young housewife.

The No. 3 DALESMAN "YORKIST"

Clarks "Avon" Gas Cooker
For description — see over.

BADDA 598

BADDA 482

SIZES	With "Yorkist" Steamless Glass Panel in Oven Door. Plain Enamel Coloured Tiles fitted. Shown with No. 3 Tiled Jamb Mouldings.		
Fire ... 14 ins.			
Solid One-Piece Cast Iron Oven, 15½ ins. wide × 17¾ ins. high.	As specified on pages 2, 3, and 4	£17 2 0	£19 10 0	£20 4 0
	Nickel Plated Bright Parts, Hot Closet Doors (Edge)	2 7 6	2 7 6	2 7 6
Size of Opening, 38 × 51 ins.	No. 3 Tiled Jamb Mouldings	4 5 3	5 3 9	5 8 9
	Ashes Pan fitted to Fret	3 0	3 0	3 0
Supplied with Oven on Right or Left-hand side.	Prepared for H.P. Boiler	4 6	4 6	4 6
	No. 1 Raised Curb Fender, 48 ins.	17 3	£1 5 6	£1 11 6
	Hearth Tiles in Plain Colours	14 0	14 0	14 0
		£25 13 6	£29 8 3	£30 13 3

EXTRAS

N.P. Parts Chromium Plated, **35/-**   Hotplate Boiling Flues, **20/-**
Best Stove Black, **13/-**   Do. Mouldings, **4/6**   Do. Curb Fender, **3/9**
Mottled Tiles to Stove, **7/9**   Do. No. 3 Mouldings, **6/-**   Do. Hearth, **9/-**
For High Pressure Boiler, pages 28 to 30. Extras, pages 27 and 31.

15

ILLUSTRATION 7

Catalogue for Clarks, about 1935
Courtesy of Clarks Stove Co. Ltd.

ILLUSTRATION 8

Catalogue for The 'Yorkist' Combination Stove, 1936, Courtesy of Baxendale & Co. Ltd

ILLUSTRATION 7 Gas cookers were more popular than electric ones as many houses only had wiring for lights. Gas was also cheaper to run and temperatures could be quickly adjusted. This 'Avon' Gas Cooker was designed for households of two or three, but larger models were available. Its grey-mottled porcelain enamel finish and white door were easy to clean. Plate racks and shelves were included.

ILLUSTRATION 8 Solid fuel stoves were still available and were very similar to traditional ranges. The No 3 Dalesman 'Yorkist' was suitable for family cooking. The glass panel in the door is a new feature as are the plain coloured tiles fitted to the surround and hearth.

ILLUSTRATION 9

The Ideal Home magazine, June 1938
© *www.timeincukcontent.com*

ILLUSTRATION 9 New suburban houses were often built with a north-facing walk-in larder, off the kitchen, which was used to keep food cool. Refrigerators were expensive and were only installed in kitchens of wealthy homes. They were generally freestanding and were likely to run on gas, bottled gas or oil. Their white exteriors implied cleanliness and hygiene.

ILLUSTRATION 10 An increasing range of electric appliances came on the market, including stylish chromium-plated electric toasters and irons. Electric saucepans and small table-top breakfast cookers were also on sale. Blue-banded Cornish Ware had, from the late 1920s, become indispensable in the stylish kitchen. Bakelite was used on many domestic goods, including this black wall clock.

ILLUSTRATION 10

The Ideal Home magazine, February 1938,
© *www.timeincukcontent.com*

*T*HIS group of interesting kitchen appliances includes the chromium plated electric toaster, £1 1s. 9d.; buff porcelain heat-controlled iron, £1 15s.; chromium plated electric saucepan, capacity 1 pt. £1 14s.; grey enamel breakfast cooker, £2 15s.; and the black bakelite kitchen clock for A.C., £2 18s.

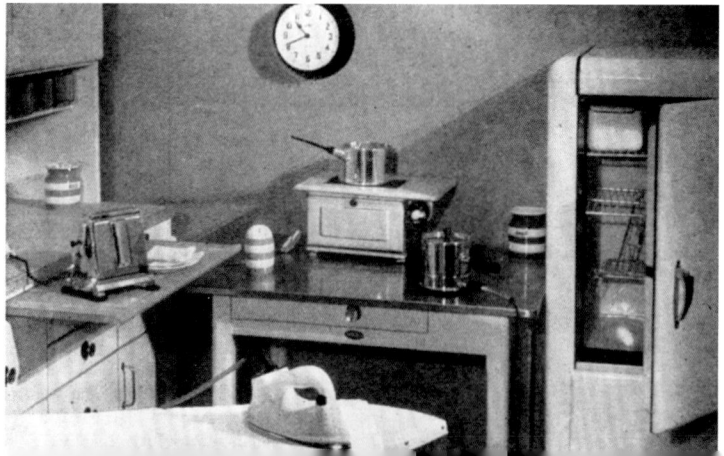

BATHROOMS

Like kitchens, bathrooms in the 1930s expressed convenience and modernity. All new middle class homes had plumbed-in, fixed baths and indoor toilets.

Cleanliness and hygiene were very important issues of the time, influencing bathroom design and layout. Hard, bright surfaces, which made a virtue of cleanliness were ideal, hence the widespread use of glazed tiles and chromium fittings. Taps, towel rails, plugs and many bathroom accessories were chrome plated. Enamelled iron baths and ceramic hand basins had easy-to-clean surfaces. Lino was a common floor covering and one that was readily maintained.

In order to make it as easy as possible to keep the bathroom sparkling, baths were enclosed by panels to eliminate the dust-collecting gaps that resulted from freestanding baths. Walls were generally tiled, at least in part. Owners tiled as high up the walls as they could afford.

Baths were generally placed in an alcove or in one corner of the room with the hand basin nearby. The toilet was often in a small, separate, adjacent room. A mirror was fixed over the hand basin, sometimes with a wall lights above or on either side. Baths and hand basins were rectangular with square edges. So too were any shelves or tables. Everything in the bathroom was functional and streamlined, reflecting concerns about hygiene.

Standard issue bathrooms in state housing and in many suburban homes were mainly white. But coloured suites were strongly marketed by the manufacturers and gave people the chance to create a more luxurious style of bathroom. The aim was to make it a co-ordinated space and a full range of matching bathroom fittings and accessories were on sale.

Pattern in the bathroom was restricted to the walls, either in the tiling or a special patterned wallpaper, and occasionally a patterned rug or lino.

SW16A

BADDA 85

ILLUSTRATION I Leading wallpaper manufacturers, such as Sanderson's, promoted the use of wallpaper in the bathroom for use above white tiling and they produced patterns specifically for this purpose. The papers often had water-related themes, such as fish or seabirds. Here a seascape border is applied to a background paper of clouds. The seagulls could be arranged as desired to complete the 'wallpaper mural'.

ILLUSTRATION 2 Tiles were widely used in bathrooms to create hygienic walls and surfaces. They were usually white or cream. Decorated or coloured tiles were used, if at all, to provide accents of colour or to introduce the occasional motif into an otherwise plain scheme. Here the wall is tiled up to door height, an expensive arrangement. A fashionable geometric pattern and 'panelled areas' have been built up from orange, green and black tiles and the whole area is edged in black.

ILLUSTRATION 4
Catalogue for Twyfords, about 1935
© Twyford Bathrooms.

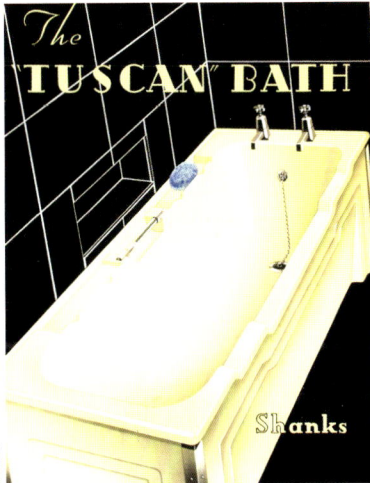

BADDA 3407

ILLUSTRATION 3
Catalogue for Shanks, 1937
© Ideal Standard (UK) Ltd.

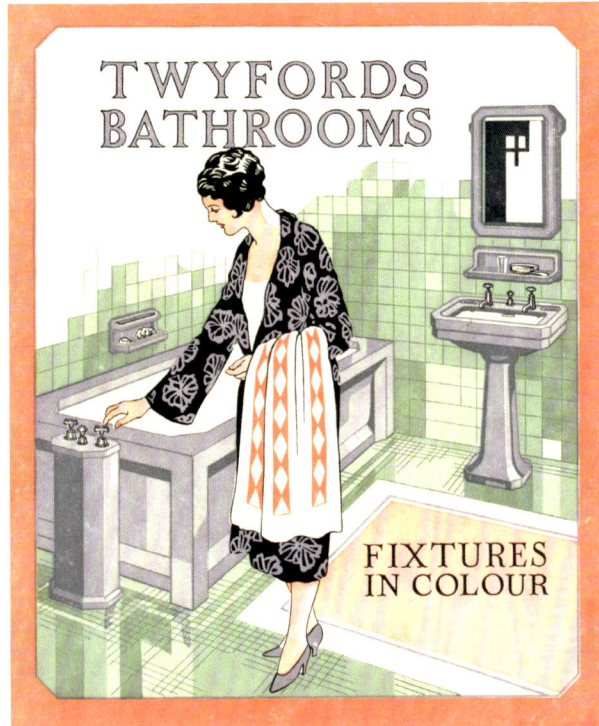

BADDA 51

ILLUSTRATION 3 Baths were boxed in with matching easy-to-clean panels. This 'Tuscan' bath has chromium plated corner strips to co-ordinate with the taps and other accessories, and a stepped rim, the shape of which is reflected in the panel. The lower rim made it easier to step into the bath as well as being visually attractive.

ILLUSTRATION 4 Coloured bathroom suites became fashionable in the 1930s and were introduced by all the leading manufacturers. Twyfords offered a choice of four colours - lavender blue, celadon green, old ivory and black. Their bathroom fittings were distinctive as the insides were finished in white.

Fig. J. 514. BOLDING's Chromium-Plated BATH SPONGE HOLDER, size 7¾ in. × 5¼ in. **19 0**

Fig. J. 516. BOLDING's Chromium-Plated BATH SPONGE and Single SOAP HOLDER, size 11¾ in. × 5¼ in. **£1 4 0**

ILLUSTRATION 5

Catalogue for John Bolding & Sons, about 1935
Courtesy of John Bolding & Sons Ltd.

ILLUSTRATION 7

Catalogue for Twyfords, about 1935, © Twyford Bathrooms.

ILLUSTRATION 6

Catalogue for Gardiner Sons, 1936, © Gardiner Sons & Co Ltd.

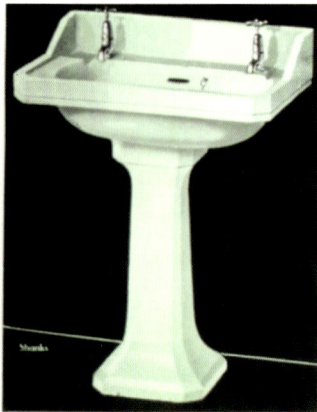

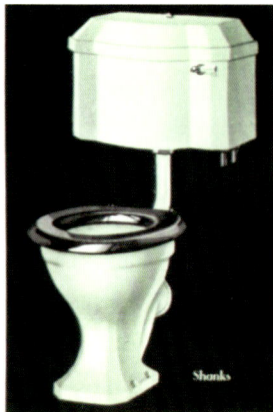

ILLUSTRATION 5 Accessories like soap, sponge and toothbrush holders were offered in different styles, colours and finishes. They were very popular in chrome to match taps, pipes and towel rails.

ILLUSTRATION 6 Hand basins, then known as lavatories, were large and rectangular, and usually raised on a pedestal though some had chrome supports at both corners of the front of the

X9618—"Trevor" Pedestal Lavatory, in

X9680—"Nisa" Low Down Closet

BADDA 226

Fig. J. 571. BOLDING's Telescopic SHAVING MIRROR, with Chromium-Plated collapsible arm reversible plain and magnifying mirror, 8 in. diameter, and screws. Full extension, 18 in. £1 17 6

Fig. J. 572. BOLDING's Adjustable Frameless SHAVING MIRROR, with metal damp-resisting back, and screws. Mirror, 7 in. diameter. Chromium-Plated ... £1 6 0

3. BOLDING's Soiled Towel Circular BASKET, in. diameter, 12 in. Chromium-Plated. ... £2 15 0

Fig. J. 574. BOLDING's cellulose enamelled Corner LINEN BASKET, on Lloyd Loom, length 20 in., side 15 in., lined with nickel-plated, gilt or oxydised copper handle.
Walnut ... Walb

ILLUSTRATION 8

Catalogue for John Bolding & Sons, about 1935, Courtesy of John Bolding & Sons Ltd

basin. Toilets were often in a separate small room adjacent to the bathroom. Low-level cisterns linked to the bowl by a chrome pipe were popular. Some, but not all, toilets had lids as well as seats and these were often black.

ILLUSTRATION 7 A large number of matching bathroom accessories were available. There were mirrors with coloured frames, bathroom cabinets, shelves and soap and sponge trays. Another possible bathroom feature was a ceramic dressing table attached to the wall by concealed brackets. Bathroom chairs and stools always had

cork seats. Taps and towel rails were usually chrome.

ILLUSTRATION 8 Extending, circular, chrome shaving mirrors were attached to the wall. Linen and towel baskets were generally either chrome plated to match the other fittings or Lloyd Loom. Made of paper, which was twisted into fibres, Lloyd Loom furniture was popular in the 1930s. Linen baskets, some with glass tops, were one of the company's most successful products and in the 1920s and 1930s were practically a standard item on British wedding lists.

ILLUSTRATION 9 Taps had a simplified, more streamlined design than seen previously and were of polished chrome. Showers were increasingly an option, although always incorporated over the bath not as a separate unit. Bath taps and hand-held showerheads were available both as separate items and in combination.

BADDA 2123

SAY 'PRESTEX' EVERY TIME

SINK TAPS

BATH TAPS

COMBINATION BATH AND HAND SHOWER SETS

Shower Baths are no longer a luxury. Peglers' Combination Bath and Hand Shower Sets have been designed to meet the ever-increasing demand for that little "extra touch of something different" in the modern house. Excellent range of

ILLUSTRATION 9

Catalogue for Building Trades, 1935-1937
© Pegler Yorkshire Group Ltd.

CORAL PINK	No. 5 IVORY	A.J.S. PASTEL GREEN	No. 5 PRIMROSE	No. 5 PINK
No. 5 BLUE	STANDARD GREEN	No. 5 GREEN	No. 145 GREEN	BLACK

COLOUR CHART

A FULL range of " Pyramid " Sanitary Earthenware is supplied in the colours shewn above. Brilliant leadless glazes in Colour reflect the same high standard of quality and finish which characterises " Pyramid " White Ware.

The Colours are permanent and are matched by leading Bath Manufacturers.

Further particulars and Coloured Earthenware samples may be had on application.

Requests for colour samples are cordially invited. A large stock of Coloured goods is always in readiness for immediate delivery.

PYRAMID COLOURED WARE

Page 5

ILLUSTRATION 10

Catalogue for JH Bean, about 1935
Courtesy of J.H. Bean & Co.

ILLUSTRATION 10 This colour chart shows some of the finishes that were available for bathroom fittings and accessories. Green, blue, yellow, pink, ivory and black were offered by most manufacturers.

ILLUSTRATION 11 Hand basins and vanity units were sometimes incorporated into the bedrooms of more expensive suburban houses. Pink was a popular colour in bedrooms generally and this extended to hand basins. Mirrors were often placed above hand basins. Here a circular mirror is set into the splashback unit.

ILLUSTRATION 11

Catalogue for JH Bean, about 1935. Courtesy of J.H. Bean & Co.

FURTHER READING

Jackson, A. (1973). *Semi-detached London: suburban development, life and transport, 1900-1939,* Allen and Unwin

Jensen, F. (2012). *Modernist Semis and Terraces in England,* Ashgate

Law, M. J. (2014). *The experience of suburban modernity: How private transport changed interwar London,* Manchester University Press

Little Palaces: house and home in the inter-war suburbs (2003), Museum of Domestic Design and Architecture, Middlesex University

Oliver, P., Davis, I., & Bentley, I. (1981). *Dunroamin: the suburban semi and its enemies.* London: Barrie & Jenkins

Ryan, D. S. (2015), *The Inter-War Home and Suburban Modernity: The Architecture, Design and Decoration of the Semi-Detached House in England.* Manchester University Press

Scott, P (2013), *The Making of the Modern British Home: The Suburban Semi and Family Life Between the Wars,* Oxford University Press

Turner, M. (1983), *The decoration of the suburban villa, 1880-1940,* Middlesex Polytechnic, London.